Sunset Lessons

Reflections on Light and Love from the Darkest of Places

Sunset Lessons

Reflections on Light and Love from the Darkest of Places

Roddy Carter, MD

Aquila Life Science Press
La Jolla, California

FIRST AQUILA LIFE SCIENCE PRESS EDITION, MAY 2020
Published by Aquila Life Science, LLC, La Jolla, CA

SUNSET LESSONS.

Printed in the United States of America

To my beloved wife Karen,

who was, is, and always will be

at the very center of my being.

Your light shines forever in my heart.

Contents

Preface

My wife enjoyed sunsets.

Actually, that's a glaring understatement. Karen truly, deeply *loved* sunsets. Any sunset. Every sunset. Those magical, fleeting moments touched her soul.

And so, we watched many of them.

In our final home together in Southern California, Mother Nature seldom disappointed, with only the occasional clouded evening obscuring the uplifting spectacle Karen so eagerly anticipated at the end of each beautiful day.

I too was deeply moved by the heavenly display of light and subtly shifting shades. But what touched me most was Karen's pure joy and uninhibited participation in the ethereal moment.

Most sunsets, I simply stood with her, seeking to suspend time to preserve the shared moment. Other times, the optical pageant offered a profound message to any willing listener, and we shared fully in the significance of the moment.

In this book, a work of unreserved devotion, I try to capture both the magic of Karen's wonder and a few of the lessons the universe extends to each of us as we watch the enchanting procession of the setting sun.

In the year since Karen died, I have continued our evening walks—at first, painfully alone and lonely, walking in a desperate attempt to find her. With each step I took, and with each setting sun, came more insight and more peace.

As the weeks and months passed, solace came in three dramatic breakthroughs. These form the backbone of this narrative. No single one is more important than the next, but I believe the sequence has been critical to my healing.

In between, a host of powerful snapshot insights illuminate the power of the setting sun and pay tribute to Karen's life and her love affair with the last rays of light that mark the end of the day.

I started this journey in the fierce grip of grief and despair. As I progressed, Karen and her setting sun taught me about life, loss, and love. And now, I am forever filled with gratitude and hope.

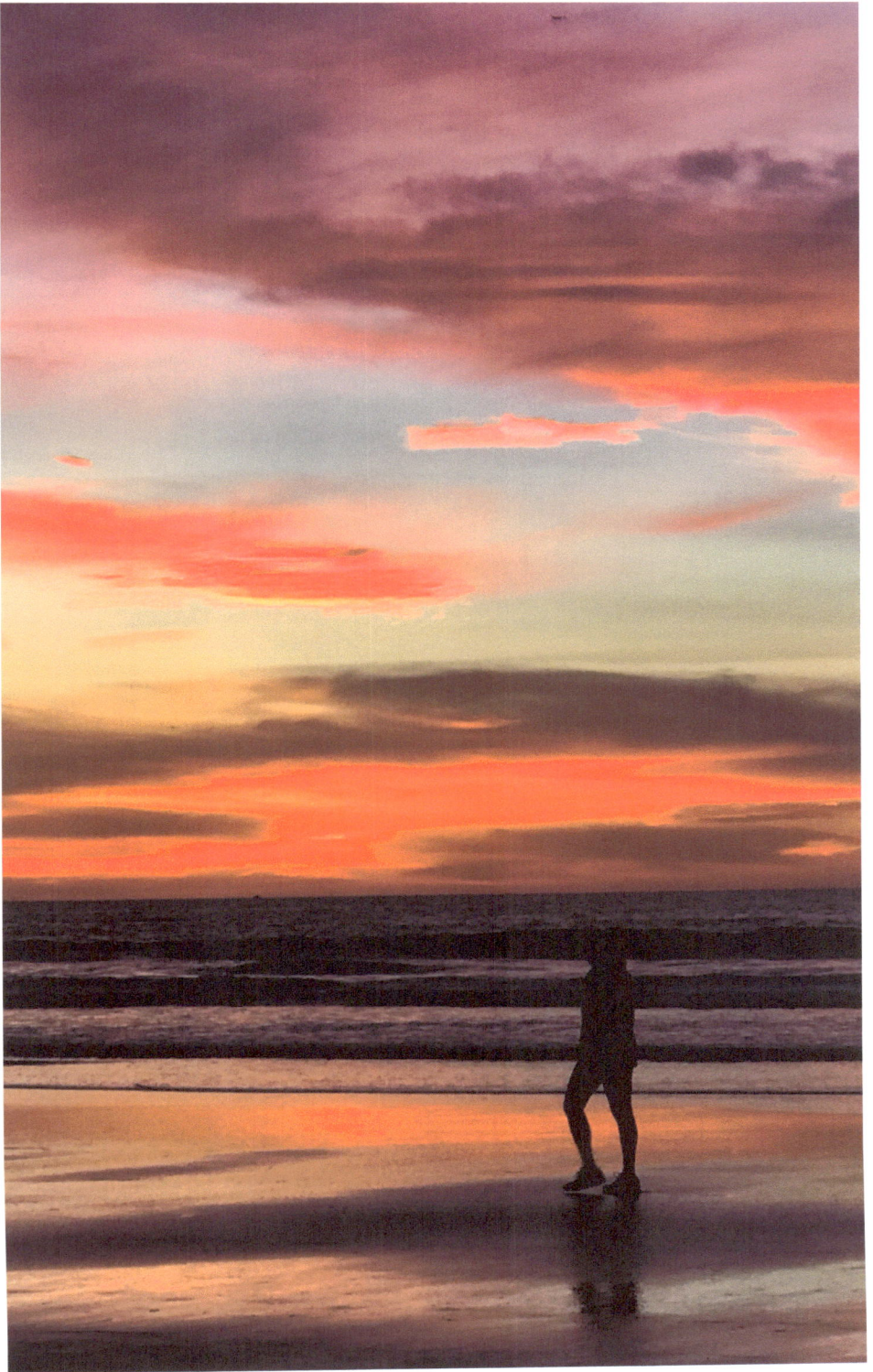

Premature
Sunset

Karen and I met at high school,

and I still clearly remember our first long walk together to watch the sunset. It was a warm summer's day, and the air was particularly clear. The sun eased lazily toward the horizon, where it met and mingled with a few wispy white clouds that scattered the orange rays, creating shadowy streaks that reached across the sky toward us. We shared long-range dreams of hope and joy as we contemplated our futures… together. Finally, the sun dropped out of view, leaving its magical after-waves to bathe the plains of Africa.

As the years passed, we walked and dreamed often, choosing dusk with its magical light as the backdrop for our shared growth: getting married, starting a family, raising our four children.

Then, after over 30 years of marriage, we received the news: Karen had cancer—advanced, metastatic cancer.

The evening of her diagnosis, we walked together, hand in hand. Silently, for the first time, we contemplated the possibility of one final sunset.

And then we began the battle of our lives.

Exceptional medical care, profound personal strength, and a deep refusal to imagine failure bought us a miraculous reprieve several years long. In very good health, we moved from Princeton, New Jersey, to San Diego, California, to live and walk on the beach of our dreams.

Magnificent sunsets ignited hope in our hearts and filled our lives with healing energy. Most days we would head down to the beach for our evening walk, hand in hand, discussing the little things in our lives.

"How was your day?"

"How did the big meeting go?"

"What are your plans for tomorrow?"

Like nearly all couples, most of our time was taken up with the little things.

On one particular day, we walked down the short road that led us to a less-known access point to the public beach. We had been living in San Diego for a few years and felt very much at home. Our health was good; our children were happy. And we enjoyed the warmth of the late-afternoon sun in our faces.

We were secure in our knowledge of local conditions by then. We could see how high the tide was without using online tide charts and knew we'd have plenty of sand to walk on that evening.

We also knew what time the sun would set. We expected an exceptional sunset that night, and we were pleased with the timing. The air was clear, and a few wispy white clouds hovered smoothly above the horizon, just enough to scatter the golden rays in spectacular fashion.

Life was good.

So, we continued with our business-as-usual conversation all the way to the end of the beach. Nothing remarkable. Just calm, content, rich everyday companionship.

We lingered a little at the halfway mark, watching a pod of dolphins fishing close to the rocks, before turning for home.

We were surprised when we noticed that those isolated clouds that had tracked our early walk had disappeared, replaced by a growing wall of dusky gray. We soon realized that we were not going to enjoy the sunset we had so confidently predicted.

The sun set prematurely that night.

Life can be like that.

When the cancer returned, we renewed our commitment to life, walking many hours together, still hand in hand, toward the setting sun. Our wall of gray rolled in on a Thursday.

In characteristic fashion, Karen was determined to go to work. She was weak, but arguing with her was nevertheless a waste of time. A deeply engaged teacher, she loved her pupils and colleagues. She was not about to abandon them.

But, for the first time ever, on that Thursday evening she did not have the energy to walk as the sun was setting. Instead, we went quietly home to rest together.

For three days, an encroaching twilight spread over us, whose sacred moments remain deeply private.

On the final Monday morning, as the earth's sun rose in a breathtaking display of pastel colors, my own sun set. As the first reflections of gentle light tiptoed across the ocean to bathe the world, an impenetrable darkness engulfed my heart.

One last breath, and the center of my universe—my soul mate, my best friend, my high school sweetheart, my wife, and the devoted mother of my four beautiful children—was gone.

The Best Is Still to Come

Most evenings, Karen and I would

walk together on the beach in front of our home in San Diego. We always timed these walks to coincide with sunset. If you joined us for dinner, you were alerted ahead of time that the festivities would start with a walk on the beach: good for the body, the heart, and the soul.

So, it was no surprise when our friends Mark and Laura joined us for dinner one evening that we all found ourselves walking on the beach at sunset.

But this was no ordinary sunset. It was one of the most spectacular I have ever participated in. As Mark is also the priest at our church, perhaps we have him to thank for that particularly heavenly experience.

As often happens, that uniquely stunning sunset evolved in three distinctive phases.

First, the full sun started to soften its light as it dipped toward the horizon. I'm not exactly sure of the physics of this magical period, but every photographer knows about the "golden hour," when the light takes on special properties toward the end of the day. Rather than illuminating us in dazzling colors, it gently bounces off us, showing us in a beauty we rarely deserve.

Next, the disk of the sun turned a deep, glowing orange as it receded in shrinking fractions below the horizon. The contagious glow spread generously across the sky, magnified and scattered into spectral brilliance by the clouds lucky enough to share in the spectacle.

I call this phase the "tourist's sunset," because, as it ends, we can always see visitors to San Diego begin to pack up their beach bags and toys, heading toward their hotels for dinner.

Our walk with Mark and Laura had only just started in time to catch these first phases of the setting of the sun. We continued on, deep in conversation, perfectly content.

Because we knew that this was only the beginning.

As happens particularly when there are clouds or moisture in the air, the sunset entered its most powerful state. Refracted waves of sunlight bent their way over the horizon, illuminating the heavens sequentially in remnant orange and yellow, followed by breath-stopping pastel shades of pink, blue, indigo, and then the lingering violet that faded gently into the dark of night.

No words could ever adequately describe this overwhelming natural phenomenon. Only the profound physiological responses reverberating deep within our bodies and the majestic echoes in the hallways of our psyches could ever do this justice.

Mark was so moved by the event that it inspired a brilliant sermon the following Sunday. But more meaningful to my family, by far, was that Mark chose to use this shared experience as the foundation for the powerful homily he gave at Karen's funeral.

To a packed church, with loving family, friends, colleagues, and students sitting or standing wherever they could find space, Mark described Nature's spectacular show the night of our walk, pointing out a powerful parallel between the setting sun and the final moments of Karen's magnificent life.

Mark then stopped, almost as the universe seems to pause after the great orb of the sun dips below the horizon, before proclaiming with gentle assertiveness, "But, the best was still to come." That most spectacular third phase of the sunset, he said, reminds us that Karen's life is not over.

This was my first great sunset lesson: **The best is still to come.**

Karen lives on in radiant glory, both spiritually and by reflection in the many lives she touched through her mortal journey.

I see her daily in our children, in their love, strength, gentleness, kindness, generosity, and humor.

I know from speaking with so many kind students and their families that she lives on in countless children and adults lucky enough to have shared her classroom, where she taught far more than mathematics.

Yes, Karen continues to shine her magnificent light into the world, reflecting off us all every day.

An Homily
to Karen

Written by Reverend Mark Hargreaves

The Psalmist says: "The heavens are telling of the glory of God."

Karen and Roddy were great walkers. They've walked all over La Jolla. It was just over a year ago that my wife and I joined them for a walk on La Jolla Shores.

I confess to not being in a great mood when I arrived at their lovely home. I had spent the afternoon trying, rather unsuccessfully, to write a sermon for All Saints Day, which is a big festival in the Church when we think of the hope of heaven. And in that afternoon, I could think of nothing to say; I had a bad case of preacher's block.

So, we arrived and headed out for a walk. This was not a gentle amble on the beach; it was an earnest attempt to get in 10,000 steps.

We got to the pier at the end of the Shores just as the sun was setting. We stood there amongst a couple of dozen people and watched the sun go down. The little crowd included a number of photographers. After the sun had disappeared over the horizon, many of the photographers left…but some stayed. I reckon that they were the locals and the professionals; they had an inkling of what was coming next.

As the sun went away, so the sky began to light up in a magnificent range of colors. It changed from red to orange to pink to blue. It was an amazing show, like a firework display in slow motion.

The heavens were telling of the glory of God.

Roddy, who knows a thing or two about these things, said it was one of the best three sunsets he had ever seen.

And I had some inspiration for my sermon. What that sunset taught me was that the going down of the sun was not the end of the sunset.

When the sun disappeared, the best was still to come. The setting of the sun gave rise to a yet more glorious scene.

What looked like an end wasn't the end. So it is with death; death is both an end and a beginning.

As Saint Paul writes, "The perishable body must put on perishability, and this mortal body must put on immortality."

It is in this hope, a hope Karen shared, that we gather this afternoon. In this service we grieve Karen's passing from us and we commit her to God's keeping in the land of light and joy, which as yet we cannot see.

What feels like an end is not the end. So, when you see a sunset, think of Karen. And think of her especially after the sun has just gone down. Make that a special "Karen moment."

And if the sky lights up, as it did for us on that beach a year ago, then take that as a promise that the best is yet to come.

"The heavens are telling the glory of God" and declaring the hope that is in us.

No Dark
Without Light

My first sunsets alone

were intensely painful.

It was true that my prevailing sentiment was deep gratitude for the life Karen and I had shared. But those early, lonely steps were tough.

I didn't want to walk alone. But although I was lonely beyond words, I didn't want to walk with anyone else, either. I only wanted to walk with Karen.

Of course, that could no longer be.

Still, I walked. And I chose to walk at sunset in the hope that, somehow, I would find her out there on the beach, floating like a mist over the ocean or carried to me on the sun's last golden rays. I hoped that, somehow, mysteriously, she would be waiting for me; that she would send me a special message that I would know without doubt was from her, just for me. I listened to the wind, in case I might hear her whisper.

There were many spectacular sunsets on those early days.

But each one ended in darkness, and I never heard her voice, or felt her touch, or saw her face in the clouds. It didn't matter how hard I tried; I couldn't find her.

The walk, the sunset, and my day always ended in darkness.

Then, one evening, as I turned for home, the darkness had a warmth to it. I can't describe more accurately how it felt different than the preceding cold darknesses. It just did.

Dissonance is a powerful hint that we're standing on the edge of an important discovery. And so I listened intently, creating mental and emotional space for the learning to emerge.

Slowly, my thoughts began to focus on that greatest of all philosophical and intellectual conundrums: the polarity dilemma, a problem that is at the same time glaringly obvious and cognitively vexing.

It is only in darkness that we fully appreciate the light. It is only in pain that we fully appreciate pleasure. It is only in the cold that we fully appreciate warmth. It is only in loss that we fully appreciate love. When we encounter the negative, we are starkly reminded of the gift of the positive.

More deeply than ever before, I was filled with immense gratitude for the life I shared with Karen. My pain was in direct proportion to the immeasurable gift of her love and companionship. If I had not had the privilege of loving her so deeply, I could not have felt her loss so profoundly.

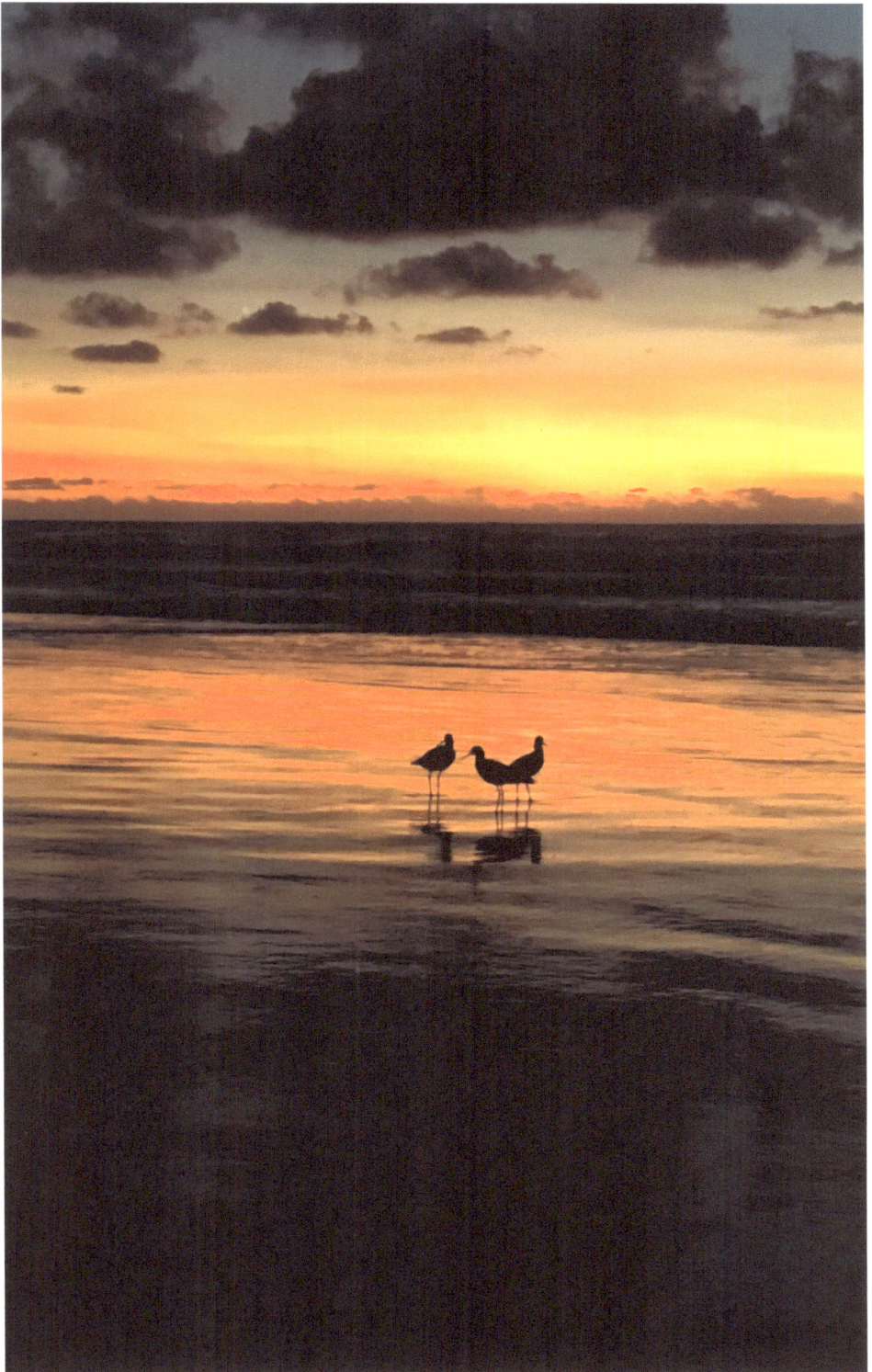

Reflected
in the Moon

Not every night was dark.

The moon was visible on many nights. Even if it was obscured by clouds, or I had to wait long hours for it to rise above the eastern horizon, or if it was a tiny crescent, or a pale shadow—still, the moon provided a little light.

Some nights, the moon rose almost as bright as the sun.

Especially on these occasions, I reminded myself that the moon is actually a dark satellite, only visible in that it reflects the light of the cosmos, particularly the sun.

I resolved to continue my search for Karen's reflected light, even through oppressive darkness.

If I was patient, and trusted, and waited in faith, I might again see powerful evidence for the enduring presence of my beloved Karen.

Ever so quietly, hope tiptoed back into my life.

The Sun Will Come Up Tomorrow

My first great sunset lesson

was that **the best is still to come.**

I knew that Karen lived on in radiant glory, both spiritually and by reflection in the many lives she touched through her mortal journey.

This insight had buoyed and inspired me through my early grief.

But I had a deep sadness and one particularly nagging realization that robbed me of peace.

There was one problem that I saw in Father Mark's homily: He'd stopped during the most beautiful phase of the sunset, the magical light that persists even after the sun has actually disappeared.

I agree that this lingering light pageant closely parallels Karen's own life. Her light continues to shine through her loved ones: family, friends, colleagues, and students.

But this wasn't my complete experience of Karen's sunset. Mark forgot to say that there is one final phase in the journey of the setting sun.

Night.

After the sunset, darkness sets in. And that darkness stays for a long time.

A short while after Karen's death, my darkness came. I spent many days in deep, black loneliness. Even today, I often find a heavy blanket of sadness draped over my shoulders.

Yes, undeniably, night follows day.

Both my parents died. And, as a physician, I have cared for many wonderful patients and their beautiful families through death. I am not unfamiliar with grief and loss.

But nothing could ever have prepared me for the loss of my soul mate.

In our everyday lives, the darkness is meant for sleeping, for rest and recovery. But there is very little rest or recovery during the dark hours of grief.

For the first time, I profoundly and personally understand the meaning of the psalmist who described the bleakness of "the valley of the shadow of death." My journey had to continue in impenetrable darkness.

Mark's wonderful homily had not prepared me for this. How could it? Only life itself can teach this lesson.

I pushed forward, certain in the knowledge that Karen would want me to continue. Certain that our children needed me. Certain that I would dishonor the woman I still love with all my being the minute

I stopped placing one foot in front of the other.

I took solace in the uplifting presence of our children and lost myself in their service. But deep inside, my world was densely shrouded in an impenetrable darkness through which I plodded painfully on.

And so, one morning after another sleepless night, I was fully awake when the sun started trickling its gentle morning rays over the high ground in the east.

Slowly, almost imperceptibly, a tiny, fragile light began to appear. I wasn't sure of its origin, but it was undeniably present.

This light continued to strengthen, ever so gently, and I began to hear the tentative song of a few birds.

The dense darkness of night gradually made way for a spectacular orange hue in the east, and it became clear to me that the sun was rising again. Before long, warm rays bathed the earth and illuminated my path.

To be honest, I had hidden from the sunrise for a while—especially on Monday mornings. But this one seemed to take control of me from deep within. The new life and energy it brought were palpable, and I was reminded immediately of one of my favorite songs, sung by little red-headed orphan Annie. Although lonely and alone, abandoned in the orphanage under the fierce and punishing hands of Miss Hannigan, the beautiful Annie looks into our souls and sings,

"The sun will come out, tomorrow.
Bet your bottom dollar that, tomorrow,
There'll be sun."

Here, right in front of me, was the next big step forward. The heavens had brought me my second great sunset lesson: **The sun will come up, tomorrow.**

Not only was the best yet to come, but even after the darkest of nights, Karen's light would rise up to warm our hearts and guide us forward in love and strength.

I found undeniable evidence of Karen's presence in this miraculous reawakening. I could walk onward again in the knowledge that moments of deep pain would be repeatedly banished by Karen's resilient and recurring presence. She knew that her voice would forever attach to the universal cycle of light and dark. Somehow, she knew that we would always find her at the end of the day, her gentle strength forever present in the setting of the sun—and in the fresh light that would bathe the earth when it rose again after the dark night.

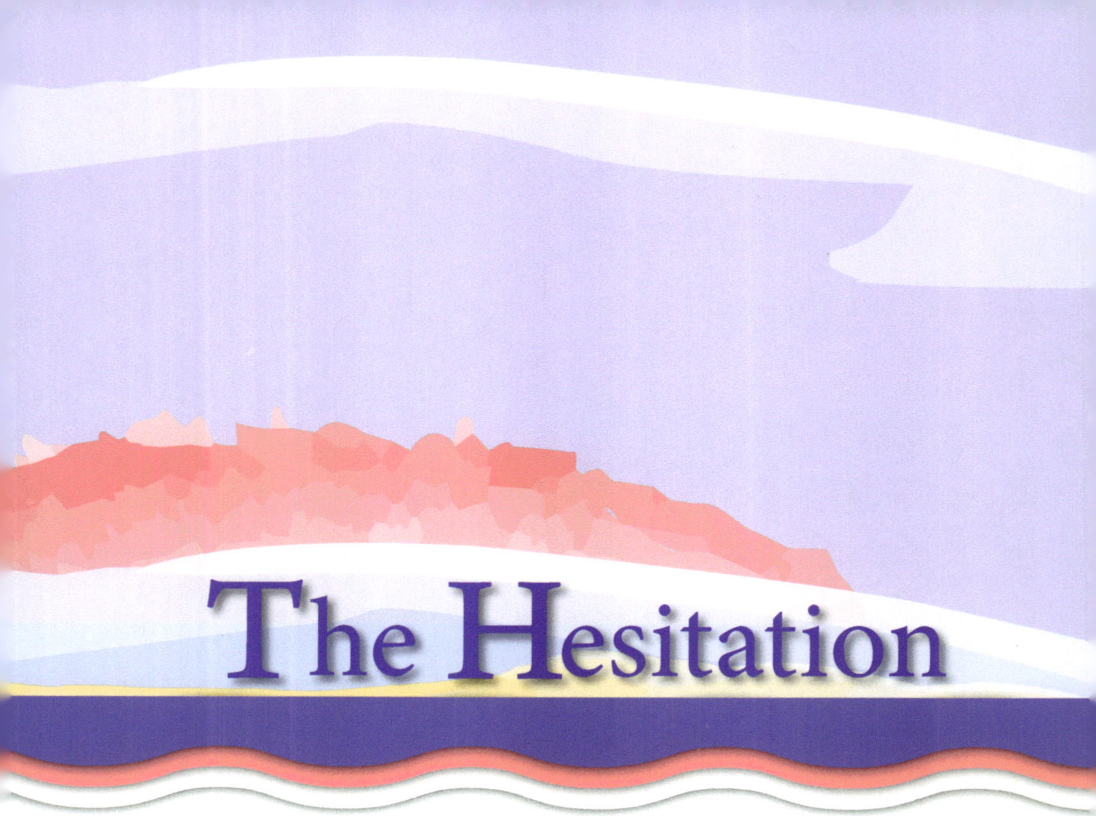

The Hesitation

Have you ever noticed that the world

seems to pause—to hesitate ever so briefly—just before the sun sets?

I know this because Karen and I used to try to predict the actual moment that the sun's circumference would disappear from view. As we walked or stood together, I would count down, first in minutes, and then in seconds. Karen always laughed, because I was always wrong. Somehow, it always took a few seconds longer than I had anticipated.

Shortly after Karen's death, I received a wonderful message from a dear friend of ours. Karen had taught her son math, and Karen had told her how, at the end of every class, this little boy stayed back. He hesitated at the door, standing out of the way as the noisy chaos erupted out of the classroom, before returning quietly to her desk.

"Thank you for teaching me, Mrs. Carter," he said.

The same line every time. Nothing more. Nothing less. Simple gratitude.

I try not to anticipate the precise moment of sunset anymore. Instead, I try to lengthen that tiny pause. I try to extend the moment of pure bliss.

Given the massive difference in cosmic scale, I would be very surprised if this ephemeral pause was designed for the sun to say thank you to us.

Instead, I like to believe that this easy-to-miss cue is a subtle reminder for *us* to hold life in our human hands with humility, reverence, and gratitude. It is *our* chance to pause to say "thank you."

Fresh Starts

We are used to thinking that,

when the sun sets, it signals an ending.

Usually, it's simply the end of the day, and before we had electricity it meant the end of work and time to settle in for the night. Many animals still have the cadence of their lives tightly linked to the rising and setting of the sun.

Karen was a schoolteacher. She was an exceptional teacher, well-loved by her students, their parents, and her colleagues. She taught mathematics her entire working life to both eager and reluctant students.

Actually, she did much more than that—she taught *life* to every child lucky enough to enter her classroom.

She worked very hard, determined to give of her best every day and in every class. So, when she came to the end of a school year, she was exhausted.

As the sun sets at the end of each busy day, I am reminded of all those last days of school that Karen enjoyed. As the final bell rang, she would say her goodbyes, pack up her bags, and wipe down the whiteboard.

This final, symbolic gesture neatly wrapped up a long year of hard work and care. With a clean slate, literally, she would turn her back on the classroom for a season of recuperation and self-care.

And after the long, lazy summer, she would return to her classroom again, filled with enthusiasm and hope for the new academic year.

This is the promise of sunset.

Each day we are invited to wipe down our own boards and turn inward to our families and ourselves. We are invited to rest and sleep. And then we are invited to awake refreshed and hopeful in the morning, with a clean slate and a heart filled with gratitude and hope, to enjoy another day.

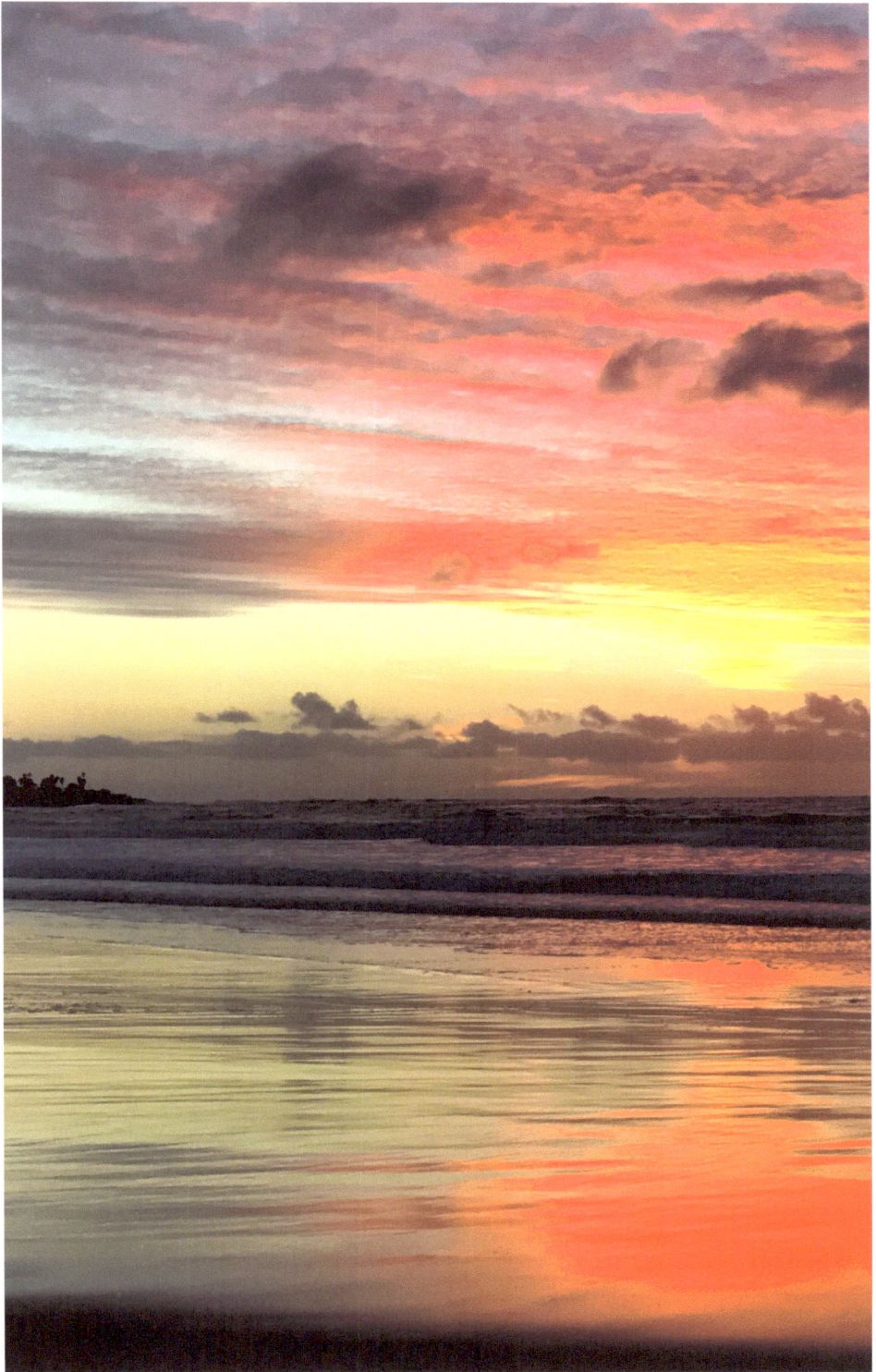

Carpe Diem

Karen lived a powerfully present life.

She always seized the day. One of her favorite movies was *Dead Poets Society*, in which Robin Williams plays a charismatic educator who inspires his students with his *carpe diem* mantra.

I was always the planner, living ahead of my time. While my head was strongly pointed at the future, Karen lived every moment given to her.

She would walk slowly, feeling the warmth of the day and the company she kept. She spent countless hours sitting inside on the carpet or outside on the grass, playing with our four amazing children as they grew into strong, confident, creative people. She loved nothing better than an afternoon at leisure, relaxing with her sisters, laughing with her brother, reminiscing with her parents.

One of the great lessons she taught me was to slow down, to stay present. I thank God that I listened to her because those slow days with her remain some of my most treasured memories.

It always struck me as somewhat surprising that she enjoyed sunset as much as she did. After all, there wasn't much day left to seize once the sun took its regular exit. And yet, she glowed with joy and excitement at sunset. Her childlike fascination could touch the hardest of hearts, and she would often dance on the beach in the glorious light, her high spirits overcoming any natural shyness.

So why the fascination with sunset?

Of course, the magical display of infinite colors touched Karen deeply. Even more, she relished the reflective instincts evoked by the setting sun. And, some of the special stories and analogies that I have captured in this little book may account for some of her enthrallment.

But none of them can adequately explain the exuberance that burst out of her in these precious moments. There had to be something more, beyond the rejuvenation promised by the impending night, beyond the clean slate and invitation to a fresh start.

There had to be something more powerful to her insight.

The most obvious answer stems from the sun's role in our solar system—the intricate web of planets and stars and the infinite spaces in between that are our human context. In this world, the sun is the source of all energy. The light energy it emits is the spectral show that the universe puts on at the end of the day, capturing our minds and focusing our attention on the western horizon.

It's not simply a breathtaking show. Without the sun's light energy, we would live in darkness. Probably, we would not even live.

And there is another energy, too, felt more meaningfully by its departure at the end of the day. Each time Karen and I stayed on the beach to watch the final curtain call of our solar queen, we couldn't help but notice that it took its heat energy with it when it left. The wet sand became cold, and we'd stand a little closer together to enjoy the warmth emanating from each other. In addition to light, the sun also shares its heat energy with us.

But that's not all.

I can explain how the sun's rays touch the skin, transmitting thermal energy to our human bodies. I can explain how the light enters our retinas, passes via our optic nerves, and excites the regions of our brains that give us vision. I can even explain how a little pulse of a hormone called dopamine is released into our bodies when we behold the magical specter of the setting sun.

But none of this can get close to explaining the deep sense of awe and profound sensory extravaganza that accompanies a particularly vivid sunset. No, our knowledge of the physical sciences lets us down there.

Which means that there is still another energy form, yet to be described by erudite scientists and curious spiritualists, that travels through our veins and ignites passion and meaning in our lives.

One day, perhaps, we will be able to define and measure this emotional and mental energy—maybe even spiritual energy.

Until then, for me, it's enough to know that they exist and cannot be explained within our current body of scientific knowledge. And if you're ever in doubt, join me for a beach walk at the end of the day, and I'll show you what Karen saw and understood.

So, where does this profound sunset lesson lead us?

First, all of life is energy. It is our most valuable fuel and currency. It drives all that we are and hope to be. Mastery in life relates intimately to our ability to understand and manage all the energy systems we have been gifted with.

Find them. Understand them. Nurture them. Enjoy them.

Be sure to apply them to grow your physical, emotional, cognitive, social, and spiritual intelligence. This is our purpose. This is the road to consciousness.

Second, energy is not finite.

The sun has been shining for an estimated 4.5 billion years. You may protest that the sun is only a star and that it is predicted to burn out in another 4.5 billion years or so. But from our tiny, unremarkable 60-million-year notch on the timeline of the universe, the lifespan of the sun may be considered infinite.

And so, energy may also be considered infinite. When we "run out of energy" in our daily lives, we simply haven't understood the concept of cosmic abundance. And don't forget, our sun and this galaxy we consider our home are but a minute speck in the infinite cosmic reality. There are energy sources beyond our own much-loved sun.

Finally, don't fall into the fatal energy trap that has contaminated modern civilization: considering energy to be only a resource. We are greedy consumers of energy, partly because we erroneously believe it is finite.

We strive to get more. We scheme and plan, sometimes deviously, to stockpile energy so that we can be stronger, more successful. We even steal energy from others to keep our own tanks full. I'm sure that you know at least one energy vampire who sucks you dry every time you interact with him or her.

But there is a funny rule that seems to apply to this "beyond-physical" energy. All the major religions and ancient wisdoms understand that we receive more only when we give away what we have.

Fulfillment in life comes not by conserving our energy, but from radiating and sharing it.

Perhaps this is the greatest of all lessons the sun teaches us.

More than simply seizing the day, Karen had a deep and natural leaning toward celebration. She celebrated life with unfiltered joy as the sunset exploded into a million rays of color at the end of the day.

It was Karen's special appreciation for the immense power of gratitude and her willingness to lose herself in the sovereignty of the moment that led her to choose sunset as her favorite time of day.

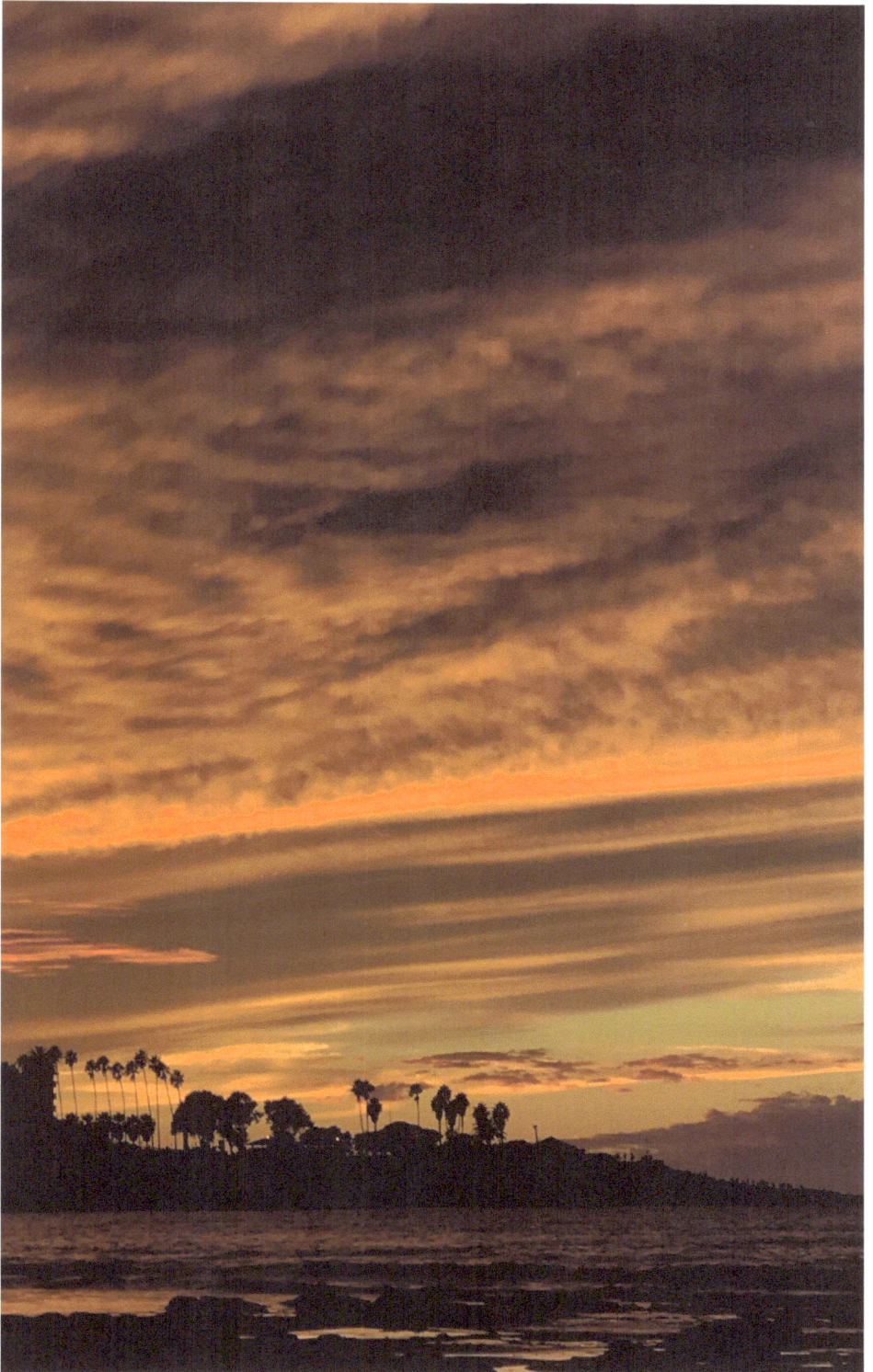

An
Endless
Sun

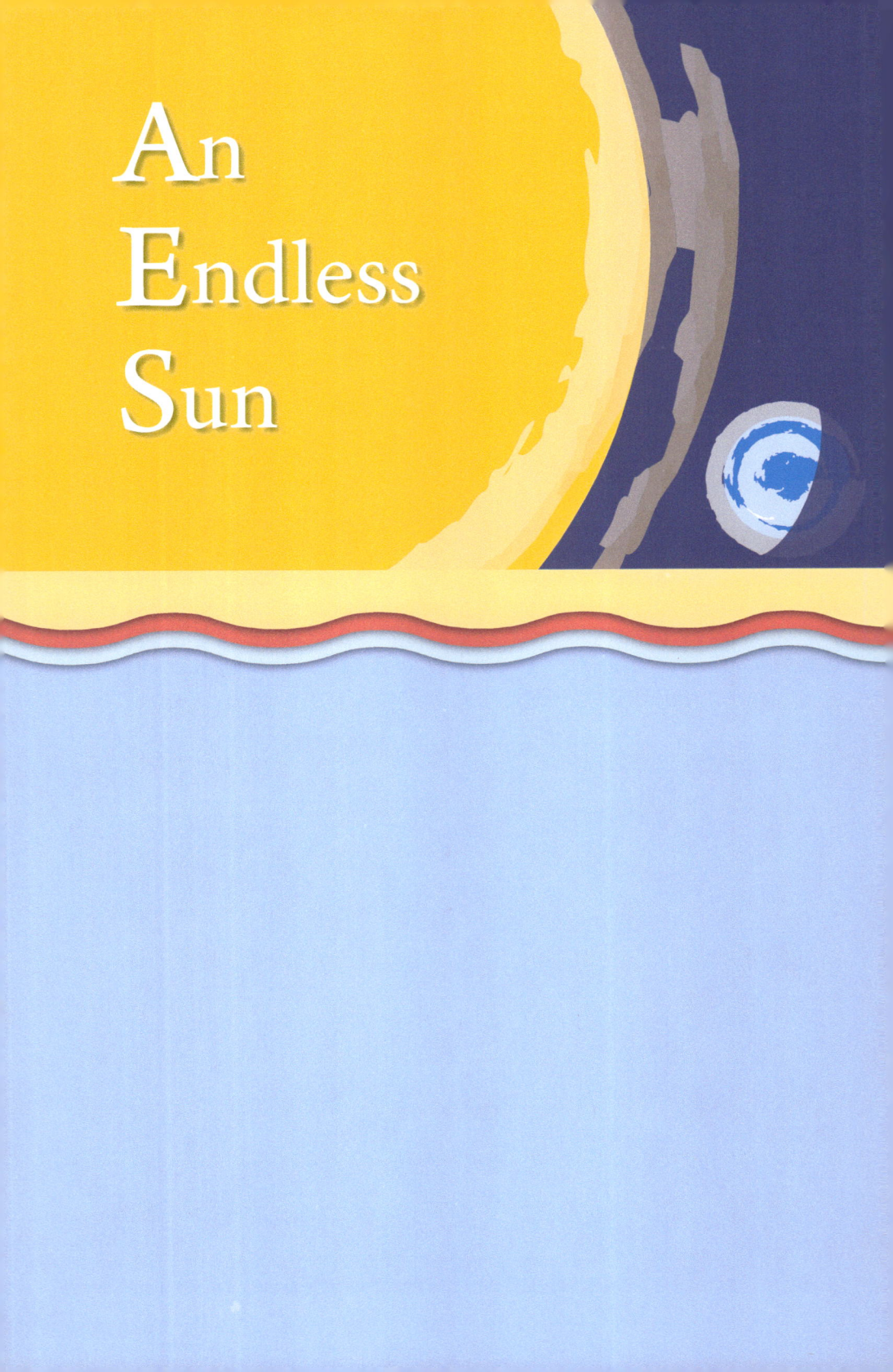

I was doing as well as could be expected.

I knew that **the best is still to come**.

The seeds that Karen planted through her life would germinate and flourish. Her four children were thriving, with her gentle fingerprints clearly visible throughout their lives. I had no doubt that countless young scholars beyond my field of view were rewarding her legacy of care and love in the classroom.

If nothing else, I knew she was at peace, no longer suffering.

I had also learned that **the sun will come up, tomorrow.** It would rise again after each long night to share its warmth and energy with our world.

We laughed often when we remembered Karen, with her colorful idiosyncrasies and her quirky way of saying things. She loved a good laugh, so we had many fond memories of her unchecked mirth. We have all kept special videos of her on our phones. In one of my favorites, you can't even see her, but in the background, you hear her infectious, irresistible laughter. For sure, her sun comes up every day in our lives in powerful ways.

But still, I struggled. I wanted these joyful memories to dominate my thoughts; not the sadness.

I was now ready for the third great sunset lesson.

I was listening to modern philosopher Eckhart Tolle speaking about the truth. "There are two versions of the truth," he announced.

This caught my attention. As an academic scientist, and a very earnest spiritual traveler, I had always been in search of *the* truth. Here was a man whose intellect I respected alerting me to the presence of two truths.

He went on to explain about the *relative truth* and the *absolute truth*. To my delight, the example he used was the sun.

The fact that the sun rises and sets every day is a relative truth: Relative to our perspective, the sun rises in the east in the morning and sets in the west each evening. During the night, the sun disappears. This is the relative truth about the sun.

But the absolute truth is that **the sun never sets**.

It appears this way to earthlings, but in truth, if you were far out in space, you would see that the sun neither rises nor sets. It shines perpetually. It never disappears.

In a flash, I had my third great lesson.

You see, as an earthling, I had been grounded in my relationship with Karen. Appropriately so. I was present with her as flesh and blood, thought and emotion. I loved this Karen with all my heart. I was totally consumed by our world and its relative truth.

And then her sun set, and she disappeared from my life. Even though she returned each day in my memories, she was nevertheless gone for long periods and in so many pervasive ways. This truth was dark and painful.

But when I am able to see the big picture, I am able to appreciate a totally different truth—one that I believe to be an absolute truth. When I create distance and perspective on my life, her life, and our lives, I notice that her light and warmth never disappear.

I can't pretend that I understand this. I can direct you to a plethora of sources, many of them religious, who will speak with authority and claim irrefutable evidence for this statement. I would lie if I told you that I had such irrefutable proof myself.

It simply feels right.

With renewed reverence for our infinite cosmic context, I see that Karen's physical absence today is only relative to my own fragile, transient mortal presence. I believe that the absolute truth is that our souls continue to journey together, intertwined and intimately united with the eternal and infinite spiritual presence that is our cosmic reality.

Today, this insight fuels my gratitude and hope.

The Green Flash

We hadn't lived in San Diego for very

long when we were exposed to a magical, almost mythical, sunset phenomenon: the green flash.

Our first awareness came when we passed a small group of sun gazers whom we now recognized as locals. "Did you see it?" they asked. Of course we'd seen it; we were only a few steps away from them as the sun dipped below the horizon. And, as customary, Karen had taken about 45 photographs of the great glowing orb and the reflected light that illuminated its trail below the horizon. How could they possibly think we'd missed it?

But the way they asked the question suggested that we may have missed something special. So, we asked what we'd overlooked.

"You didn't see the green flash?" they responded.

Now we felt stupid. A green flash? Who could miss *that*? And what was it, anyway? And now they knew we were still tourists, and not yet locals. And so, on that cool evening, we started to search for the elusive green flash.

At first, our research produced a range of divergent opinions. Did it exist, or was it a mirage? Could only some people see it, suggesting that it had more to do with our optical powers than the laws of physics? Some articles even proposed that it was only "seen" by optimistic dreamers who'd bought into a myth and then subsequently enticed their faculties to imagine the dramatic visual phenomenon.

Confused but hopeful, we set out to find the mysterious green flash for ourselves.

It didn't take long.

At first, although sure that we'd noticed it, we doubted ourselves. Had we too been deceived by the widely held myth?

But it happened too often to be the result of our imaginations. Before long, we were not only sure that we were observing a true phenomenon, but we were able to talk about variations in the quality of each flash.

If you've never seen it, you should look for it.

Physicists are now in agreement that the green flash is a spectral phenomenon produced as the sun's rays travel through the thick layer of atmosphere closest to the earth. The sun's light is scattered into its rainbow components, and for precisely 1.4 seconds, as the upper rim of the sun slips below the horizon, our eyes are able to see brilliant green rays of light.

You won't see the flash with every sunset. We require specific environmental conditions to magnify the light for it to be visible to the normal human eye. And it's theoretically visible at sunrise too, but even fewer people have enjoyed that gift.

Since Karen's death, I mostly experience the green flash alone, and my experience has become enlivened by a deep spiritual significance.

Somehow, the cosmos gave me answers as to where Karen has "gone." She hasn't gone anywhere. She is somehow here…always has been and always will be…just as the sun never sets.

The green flash tells me something about this phenomenon we call death.

Karen had her own ethereal moment as she departed this mortal life. In her last seconds, she was enveloped by peace, and a bright smile lit up her face. She even laughed very quietly—her joyful last words… her own green flash. Then, held tightly in my arms and surrounded by our children, she took her last breath, and her spirit left her body.

Like the sunset that reaches a tipping point, Karen had reached a very special moment on her journey. No longer fully present in the physical domain, which is our everyday reality, she had crossed over into the spiritual.

Today, each time I watch the green flash over the Pacific Ocean, I'm reminded that our mortal life is but a chapter in an eternal journey in which we are all seamlessly connected, with no separation and no goodbyes.

I'm truly grateful that I could share in this vivid moment on Karen's timeless journey: her own spectacular flash of enlightenment and her instantaneous release to eternal peace.

The Full Spectrum

Of course, if we spend the evening

waiting only for that vivid green flash, we lose the full power of the mystical sunset experience. Sunset's full majesty is in the breadth, depth, and diversity that Mother Nature projects across the heavens for our delight and gratification.

Most of us can list the colors of the rainbow, and if you watch carefully, you will notice the sky shifting from red to orange to yellow to green to blue to indigo and ultimately to violet before it becomes dark again.

But, in truth, real life is far richer, far more complex than this. Each of these discrete colors is only a momentary stopping place as the universe plays on its infinite optical keyboard. In between each of these famous colors are an infinite array of delicate, less-known shades. Although our cognitive brain and naming skills let us down, each and every one of these subtle shifts and gentle tones is registered deep within our hearts. This is the nature of awe.

And this is how Karen lived her life.

She not only relished a broad, deep life, with many interests and talents; she was particularly open to the immense gift that is awe. She opened her heart to every subtle color in this magnificent journey we call life, savoring every moment. Like the sun, she took her time to appreciate the enormous power of the many sensual continuums with which we humans have been gifted.

And, like watching the setting sun, if you slow down to her pace, you too will find unimaginable riches in unexpected places.

Next time you're on the beach during sunset, don't rush off as soon as the golden ball drops out of sight. Stay. Walk slowly. Perhaps you, like she and I did so many times together, will be consumed by the bold orange colors on the western horizon, only to look up and suddenly notice the surprising, subtle pastel shades in the lengthening darkness in the east that are rich optical reflections of our majestic setting sun.

Her Reflected Glory

Most people are frustrated by clouds.

Unless you're a farmer, you're likely to see them as nuisances that interrupt the beauty of broad blue skies. I'm sure you are familiar with the phrase "silver lining." The popular view is that clouds represent the undesirable, and we are taught to look hard to find something good in them.

But not when the sun sets. It's often the clouds that turn a regular sunset into a moment of awe, something more nuanced and memorable. Sunlight that reflects off the clouds takes on supernatural colors: a natural phenomenon that resonates deep within the human psyche.

I was watching one of these dramatic cloud-boosted sunsets recently, feeling Karen's closeness. The sun was well below the horizon, but its transfixing light was scattered across the sky, reflected by the clouds.

I was struck by the similarity between this dazzling, reflected festival of light and Karen's life.

Many people appreciated Karen's light and energy—a deeply moving observation in its own right. But what made her truly magnificent was the way her light reflected off the people around her.

A passionate and committed educator, she enhanced the lives of thousands of young learners. More powerfully, her deep maternal affection and unwavering devotion illuminated the lives of our children. Most intimately, she profoundly enriched my own life.

Her reflection off these human clouds remains a dazzling display of beauty, courage, hope, and promise that will endure well beyond the fading of her own mortal light.

Karen's reflected glory holds a lesson for all of us to consider: Who will reflect your glory? Entrust them with your life-giving light in the sure knowledge that they will magnify your aura unselfishly, spreading beauty and love throughout the world.

And what will you do today to reflect the glory of others? Like those "undesirable" clouds, simple folk like you and I become meaningful, even spectacular, when we work to find and share the beauty of the people with whom we are privileged to share the journey of life.

Always With Me

It has been a full year since

the premature death of my beloved Karen.

I have searched for her every single day. To be honest, I have still not found her the way I had hoped or expected.

I don't understand the full truth or the nuances of her death, and I have yet to complete the grieving process…although I strongly doubt that it's a metamorphosis with a hard stop.

So I don't pretend to have all the answers.

But I have learned a lot on my journey, and so much of this discovery came from perpetuating Karen's deep fascination with the setting sun.

I've written of these things trusting that they will give insight and hope to at least one person who today is grieving, or may be anticipating with fear, the loss of a loved one.

Death is the final chapter in our mortal experience, but that experience is only a small part of an infinite journey.

I have lived through this chapter with my soul mate. We were never more in love than during our last days together. My greatest prayer is that every human being knows for at least a fleeting moment the beauty of the intense love that I have received and given during this phase of my journey.

I have traveled through intense darkness in the valley of the shadow of her death. Slowly, light began to reenter my life. Three massive breakthrough insights enabled the gradual illumination of my soul through the fissures in my broken heart. And I have come to appreciate anew Father Mark's prophetic words: "the best is yet to come."

Today, I truly live with intense gratitude and eternal hope.

In her fascination with the setting sun, my beloved Karen led me to understand, or at least appreciate, the infinite power and pleasure that we have been given within our tiny place in the great cosmos.

I could never adequately capture my gratitude for all that Karen and the sun have taught me. The setting sun will forever remind me of Karen's recurring beauty and power. My mission is now to honor, celebrate, and perpetuate her light every day for the rest of my life.

And like the sun, Karen has not disappeared. She remains in a state of spiritual permanence, as infinite as the cosmos, with no beginning and no end.

She is always with us.

She is always with me.

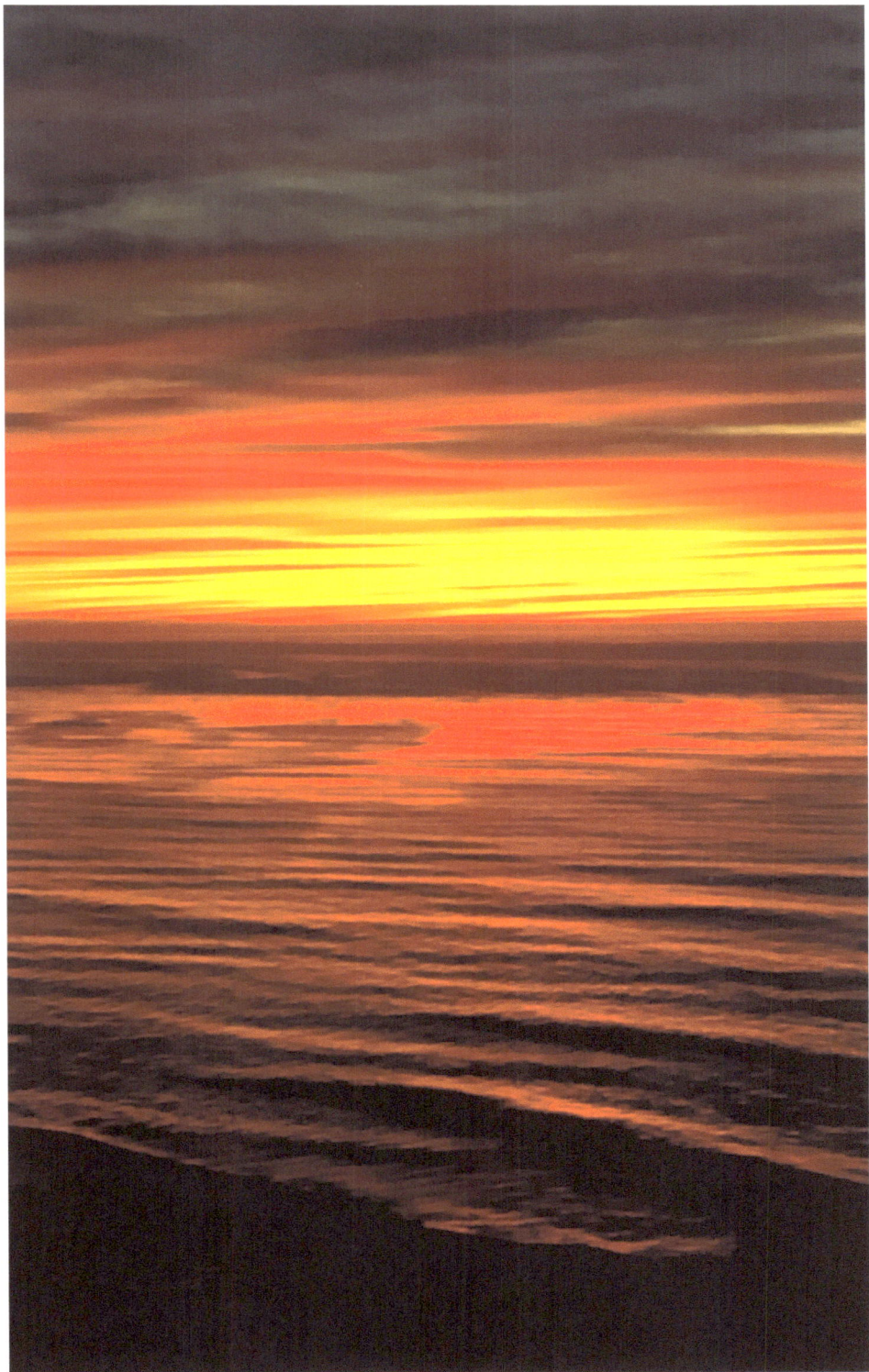

All I Need
and Love

We took this photograph on the beach at sunset less than two weeks before Karen died. She posted it to her Facebook page.

Few words mean more to me than her simple inscription, which I will forever echo with every ounce of my being.

Karen Carter is with **Roddy Carter**.

October 26, 2018 · 🌎

Got all I need and love....

18 Comments

You, Kirstin Carter and 141 others

👍❤️

❤️ Love   💬 Comment   ↪ Share

KAREN LESLEY CARTER

Karen was born in Johannesburg, South Africa, the firstborn child of Les and Denny, whose devotion provided her foundation for a life of profound value. She grew in love and later friendship with her sisters Debbi and Heidi and her brother Rogér. Despite her instinctive responsibility as the oldest sibling, she was always best known for her enduring sense of fun.

Karen emerged as a self-driven, disciplined, and honest learner during her school years. She was a nationally recognized gymnast and an enthusiastic swimmer.

Karen's parents enrolled her at St John's College for her final year of high school, where we met on the first day of school. Inseparable from the age of seventeen, we chose to go to university together. She graduated with a science degree and then pursued her post-graduate studies in math education. She fell in love with this primal discipline, recognizing the central role that mathematical logic plays in the creation of the Universe and all the other physical sciences. She returned to teach at St John's as the youngest chair of the math department— and the first woman chair in an era when male leadership enjoyed weighty domination.

Karen's legacy of integrity, compassion, and purpose lives on in the thousands of fine young women and men she taught on two continents, including at Princeton Academy of the Sacred Heart and Stuart Country Day School of the Sacred Heart in Princeton, New Jersey, and Bishop's School in San Diego, California.

MAY 1963   NOVEMBER 2018

Even more than for her professional contribution, Karen will forever be re-membered for her selfless loyalty, her bountiful passion, her care for others, and her un-complaining, unyielding strength. These traits were no more clearly evident than in her role as a loving and affectionate mother to our four children: Matthew, Michael, Kirstin, and Robyn.

Karen was the most devoted mother that any child could hope for. When our children were little, she would spend hours on the floor, just playing with them. When they were older, she spent many more hours sitting up late at night with them while they toiled over their homework.

Together, Matthew, Michael, Kirstin, and Robyn carry with them Karen's courage and keen sense of justice, her curiosity and strength, her tenderness and tenac-ity, and her creativity and sensitivity. Her spirit lives on in them.

If this book resonated with you, I'd be honored if you'd leave a review on the site where you purchased it...your voice helps others find it.

www.ingramcontent.com/pod-product-compliance
Lightning Source LLC
Chambersburg PA
CBHW041917260326
41914CB00014B/1484